IMAGES
of America

NAVAL SUBMARINE BASE
NEW LONDON

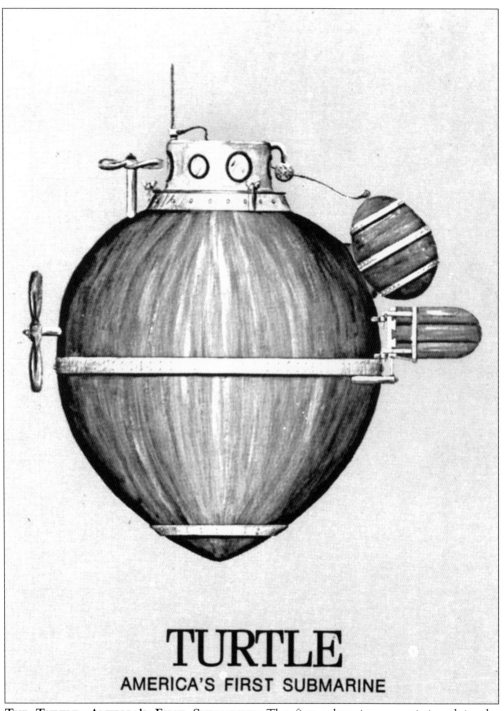

TURTLE
AMERICA'S FIRST SUBMARINE

THE *TURTLE*, AMERICA'S FIRST SUBMARINE. The first submarine commissioned in the U.S. Navy was the USS *Holland* (SS-1) in 1900. Some 125 years earlier, the *Turtle*, built by David Bushnell of Saybrook, Connecticut, was used against the British off Governor's Island in New York. (Painting by the author.)

IMAGES
of America

NAVAL SUBMARINE BASE
NEW LONDON

David J. Bishop

ARCADIA
PUBLISHING

ISBN 978-0-7385-3808-2

Published by Arcadia Publishing
Charleston SC, Chicago IL, Portsmouth NH, San Francisco CA

Printed in the United States of America

Library of Congress Catalog Card Number: 2005922440

For all general information contact Arcadia Publishing at:
Telephone 843-853-2070
Fax 843-853-0044
E-mail sales@arcadiapublishing.com
For customer service and orders:
Toll-Free 1-888-313-2665

Visit us on the Internet at www.arcadiapublishing.com

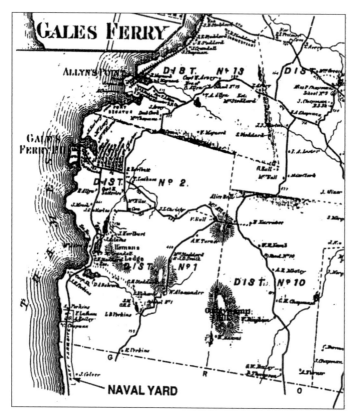

MAP OF 1868. The lower left corner shows the area designated as the navy yard, with the town line between Ledyard and Groton bisecting the site. (Courtesy of SFL&M.)

CONTENTS

ACKNOWLEDGMENTS

The assistance given me by two staff members of the Submarine Force Library and Museum (SFL&M) at the U.S. Naval Submarine Base New London contributed greatly to the creation of this book. I wish to thank museum archivist Wendy Gulley for pointing me in the right direction toward numerous rows of shelves containing photographs and histories of submarines and the base. I am grateful also to museum curator Steve Finnigan, who assisted with research and generously passed this project on to me. Their efforts over the years have made the SFL&M the premier repository for submarine history and related subjects. Additional thanks go to Erva Beard, engineering technician, and Dana Manfredi, civil engineering technician, both in the Submarine Base Public Works Department, Engineering Division, for their assistance with information regarding building numbers, construction dates, locations, and maps. As a former member of the Engineering Division team, I know firsthand of their dedication to the mission of the submarine base and their helpfulness to personnel and contractors who approach them.

INTRODUCTION

In 1799, the federal government proposed to establish a national depot for the construction, repair, and safekeeping of the U.S. Navy. Senior naval officers including Commodores Hull, Rogers, and Decatur, as well as Capt. John Paul Jones, recommended the port of New London as the proper site for such a station. It was not until 1862, however, that the first steps were taken to establish a naval station there. Secretary of the Navy Gideon Wells of Norwich, Connecticut, appointed a naval committee to consider the matter. League Island in Philadelphia was instead recommended by the committee.

On June 27, 1862, a meeting was held in the New London courthouse. Many prominent citizens gave their views, and resolutions were passed "requesting Congressman Augustus Brandegee to use all the power and influence he could muster to have the Naval site fixed in New London."

Congress also appointed a commission to investigate the harbors of three East Coast cities: Philadelphia, Newport, and New London. By a two-thirds majority, the commission voted for New London and submitted its report back to Congress. A political struggle ensued, with Secretary Wells continuing to favor League Island. Private citizens of New London spent weeks in Washington, assisting Congressman Brandegee in obtaining support for the Connecticut site. Although League Island was favored by Wells, Brandegee was able to attach a rider on the Naval Appropriations Act of March 2, 1867, which bore fruit in the establishment of a yard on the Groton side of the Thames River.

From March 1867 to April 1868, the state of Connecticut, in conjunction with the city of New London, pursued the establishment of the naval station. In summary, the state legislature appropriated up to $15,000, and the city of New London authorized, by town meeting, to appropriate up to $75,000 to purchase land to be deeded to the federal government. Local commissioners, headed by John R. Bolles, obtained options, then purchased part or all of the large farms of Jonathan Colver, Solomon Perkins, and Courtland Chapman and all of the small parcels of land owned by Frank Latham, George Anson Bailey, and Rhode Marshall. The commissioners laid out the desired site and, on April 11, 1868, presented the deed of gift to the secretary of the navy, none other than Gideon Wells. It should be noted that Bolles obtained options to purchase land on both side of the Thames River, with the idea that the navy yard would be established on the New London side.

The entire area of the reservation turned over to the navy totaled about 112 acres, covering a strip parallel to the riverfront one mile long and about 700 feet wide. At approximately the middle point, the Groton-Ledyard town line crossed the reservation from east to west, so that about half of the area was located in each town. The land was mostly level along the river's shore, with a ridge just east of the naval area.

One

THE NAVY YARD AND SHIPS

On July 19, 1868, Commo. Timothy A. Hunt took charge of the new station, becoming its first commandant, a title then preferred by the navy to recognize the commanding officers of vessels or squadrons. Over the next 47 years, the station had 26 commanding officers of various rank. Rear Adm. Oscar R. Stanton, commanding in 1898, was the most senior. Ranks of other commanding officers included captains, lieutenants, chief petty officers, and even a pay clerk.

The term "navy yard" was loosely used when referring to the base at that time. It was used as a depot for dry docking and laying-up ships when not in service. A large dry dock, the first facility employed at the base, arrived on July 2, 1869, and was used until 1875, when it settled in the mud and was dismantled.

A number of tugs, dispatch boats, and other small craft provided services here. The USS *Nevada*, USS *Severn*, and USS *New Hampshire* are among the more notable ships that were stationed at New London. The *Nevada* was laid up here between 1871 and 1873. The *Severn*, a wooden sloop-of-war, arrived on July 4, 1874, and was transferred on January 28, 1877. The *New Hampshire* was originally named the *Alabama*. After the Civil War, the vessel became the flagship for Commo. Stephen B. Luce's Apprentice Training Squadron. It arrived here on October 12, 1890, and served as a receiving ship until decommissioned on June 5, 1892.

THAMES NAVY YARD.

EARLY SHIPS AT THE NAVY YARD. The USS *Nevada* (formerly the *Neshaminy*) is laid up at a pier during 1871–1873. It was later towed to New York for breaking up. At the right is the monitor USS *Dictator* (in ordinary). It was recommissioned in New York in January 1874. (Courtesy of SFL&M.)

Two

THE DWELLINGS

Three houses were located on the property at the time of the original conveyance. They were on the west side of the State Road near the northern end of the reservation, meaning they all stood in Ledyard. Frank Latham occupied the northern house and the next one was occupied by G. A. Bailey. Each was about 75 feet west of the road and about one and a half stories high. Occupied by Courtland Chapman, the third house was larger (at two and a half stories), was closer to the river, and was about 300 feet from the road. The Chapman property included several hundred acres to the east, reaching as far as the present state Route 12, and was acquired by John Bolles. After Bolles turned the chosen acreage over to the navy, he kept the remaining 200 acres and moved the Chapman house to it. In 1911, this property was sold to the Philadelphia Breakwater Company, and a large quarry was started there. The property was later sold to William E. Dampier of New York.

A portion of the Solomon Perkins property was in the 1868 navy grant, but not the house located over the northern boundary line. South of the reservation, a cluster of about 10 houses made up the little hamlet of Mamacoke. Property owners included W. Chapman, D. Chapman, Alexander W. Milkey, S. Chapman, S. A. Chapman, and W. Lamphere. These lots were all centered around an icehouse, where ice cut from nearby Crystal Lake was stored, and a wharf, where it was delivered to fishing boats.

SOLOMON PERKINS HOUSE. This stately home belonged to Solomon Perkins at the time of the 1868 land purchase. Located just over the northern boundary of the navy yard, it was not part of the purchase, but much of the Perkins acreage was. (Courtesy of SFL&M.)

REAR VIEW OF PERKINS HOUSE. The remaining Perkins acreage and house were purchased by the Philadelphia Breakwater Company in 1911. (Courtesy of SFL&M.)

QUARTERS C. Built in 1874, this large house was located near the waterfront, facing east to the State Road. When the railroad laid tracks along the waterfront in 1899, it was moved across the State Road and turned 180 degrees, now facing west. (Courtesy of SFL&M.)

JONATHAN COLVER FARM. This group of buildings made up the Jonathan Colver property, later owned by his son Courtland Colver. The large acreage extended to the Thames River. (Courtesy of SFL&M.)

COLVER HOUSE. The main house later became a nurses' residence. (Courtesy of SFL&M.)

VIEW OF COLVER PROPERTY. Here, a chicken coop is visible to the left, and a two-and-a-half-story dwelling is to the right. (Courtesy of SFL&M.)

COLVER TOOLSHED. This building, located to the south of the two-and-a-half-story house, served as a toolshed. (Courtesy of SFL&M.)

ANOTHER DWELLING. This house stood on the eastern portion of the Colver property. (Courtesy of SFL&M.)

SMALL BUILDING. This tiny house was located to the west of the two-and-a-half-story house. (Courtesy of SFL&M.)

COLVER'S POND. After the navy purchased the property in 1941, this body of water became Rock Lake. (Courtesy of SFL&M.)

MAMACOKE HAMLET. Traveling south on the old State Road, one came upon a group of houses known as Mamacoke Hamlet. As the road made a sharp left and then proceeded south, this house was facing east. Part of the State Road was removed due to the proximity of the railroad tracks, and an upper road was created. (Courtesy of SFL&M.)

ALONG THE BOUNDARY. This house stood on the upper road facing west. The southern boundary fence and the enlisted men's barracks, Building 83, are to the left in this 1941 photograph. (Courtesy of SFL&M.)

GROUPING OF THREE. These three buildings were located across the street from the house in the previous photograph. The road to the right led to the lower State Road. (Courtesy of SFL&M.)

MORE HOUSES. These houses stood south of the preceding group of three, along the upper road. The one to the right had been moved to the new main gate by 1944; later, it was moved near the officers' club. (Courtesy of SFL&M.)

ACROSS THE STREET. Some distance from the road, this house was located across the street from the previous houses. (Courtesy of SFL&M.)

KATZ AND KAUFMAN, NAVAL TAILORS. South of the houses facing east was this building, which also included Jakes Liberty Store. (Courtesy of SFL&M.)

VIEW FROM SUBMARINE BASE. After the expansion of 1919, the old State Road was straightened, following the railroad tracks. New houses were built, as seen behind the cars. (Courtesy of SFL&M.)

JAMES R. HUNT PROPERTY. A filling station and trading post are shown on the eastern side of the straightened State Road in this 1941 photograph. At the far left is the submarine base's southern boundary fence. The front of the house to the right is pictured in the top photograph on page 17. (Courtesy of SFL&M.)

Traveling South on State Road. Just past the filling station and to the right of the large tree is the house pictured on page 18, fronting on the upper road. The white house, belonging to Mollie Sullivan, features steps leading to the new section of the State Road. (Courtesy of SFL&M.)

House on Upper Road. To the left of this house is the south boundary fence for the mine depot. To the right is Crystal Lake. (Courtesy of SFL&M.)

ADDITIONAL SULLIVAN PROPERTY. This house, also owned by Mollie Sullivan, stood south of the previous dwelling. Taken in 1941, the photograph shows buildings and a boundary fence to the right. (Courtesy of SFL&M.)

LAST HOUSE ON UPPER ROAD. The Sullivan house, located at the junction of the upper road and lower State Road, is shown in this additional view. In the distance, at the end of the upper road, is the enlisted men's barracks, Building 83. (Courtesy of SFL&M.)

PROPERTY OF NEW YORK, NEW HAVEN, AND HARTFORD RAILROAD. This house is located just south of where the upper road merged with the State Road (foreground). Behind the house, the mine depot is to the left, and Crystal Lake is to the right. This 1941 photograph shows the house after it was purchased by the railroad, along with other properties along the track. (Courtesy of SFL&M.)

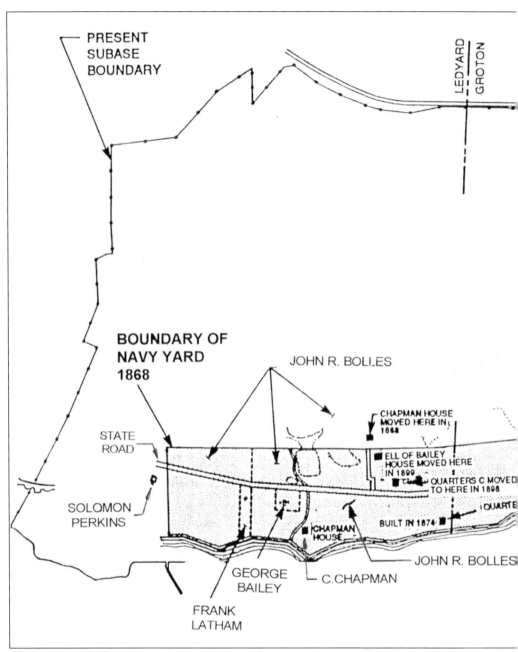

HISTORICAL MAP OF 1868. This map reveals the original navy yard land acquisition, as well as many of the houses on and around it. The present waterfront piers and northern, eastern,

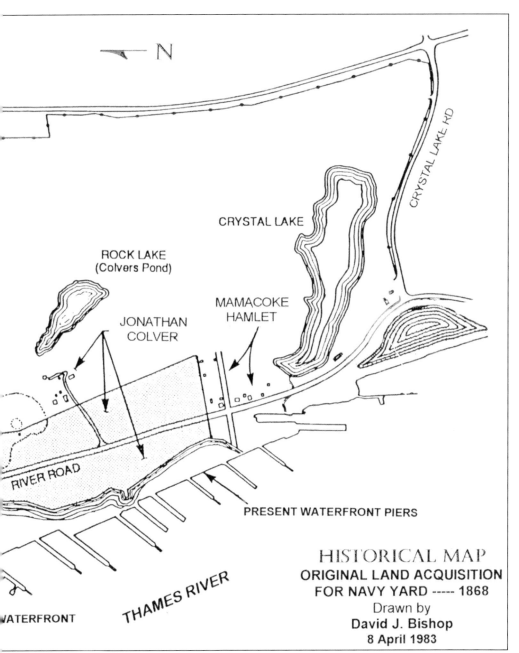

← N

CRYSTAL LAKE RD

CRYSTAL LAKE

ROCK LAKE
(Colvers Pond)

MAMACOKE
HAMLET

JONATHAN
COLVER

RIVER ROAD

PRESENT WATERFRONT PIERS

HISTORICAL MAP
ORIGINAL LAND ACQUISITION
FOR NAVY YARD ----- 1868
Drawn by
David J. Bishop
8 April 1983

WATERFRONT

THAMES RIVER

and southern boundary lines are included to help show the location of the 1868 purchase in relation to the submarine base today.

GANETTA PROPERTY. The house and buildings of Rocco and Bernadetta Ganetta are shown in this 1941 photograph. To the left is the old State Road and part of the house on page 23. In the foreground lies Crystal Lake Road. When purchased by the navy in 1941, this property became the new (and present) main gate to the submarine base. Crystal Lake is shown to the right. (Courtesy of SFL&M.)

Three

THE NAVY YARD AND BUILDINGS

In 1870, Congress made the first federal appropriations of $10,000 for the construction of docks for use in laying up ships in ordinary (protective storage). The pier was later expanded to a T shape of 800 by 50 feet and remained in use for over 50 years. Building 1, constructed in 1873, remains the oldest structure built after the navy had acquired the land. In the early days, it served as a warehouse, but it is most known as the headquarters of the base commanding officer, continuing in this capacity until 1974. Located approximately 50 yards from the river, Building 1 provides an excellent view of many of the piers. Building 2, standing to the east of Building 1, was completed in 1874. It also served as a warehouse and an administrative office. Both buildings are 100 feet long, 40 feet wide, and two stories high.

By 1881, the station consisted of five or six structures and a large pier. Other than laying up ships in ordinary, activities at the site slowly dwindled. Building 3 was erected in that year as a one-story drill hall for naval apprentices. Hopes of establishing a training facility here were dashed when Commodore Luce decided that Newport, Rhode Island, was the best site. Years later, in 1908–1909, a second story was added to Building 3 when it was used as a school for marines. This school was moved to Philadelphia in 1911.

FIRST BUILDINGS. Building 1 (right) was built in 1873 and was originally used as a warehouse. Building 2 (left), also a warehouse, was completed in 1874. (Courtesy of SFL&M.)

BUILDING 3. Originally built as a one-story structure in 1881, Building 3 acquired a second story in 1909, when it became a school for marines. (Courtesy of SFL&M.)

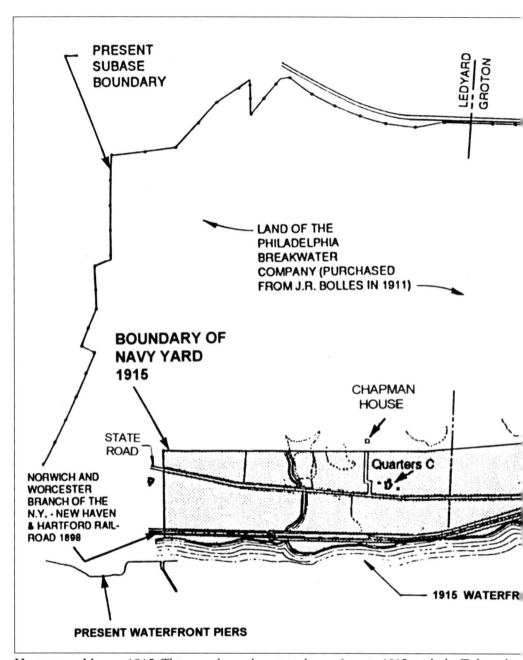

PRESENT
SUBASE
BOUNDARY

LEDYARD
GROTON

LAND OF THE
PHILADELPHIA
BREAKWATER
COMPANY (PURCHASED
FROM J.R. BOLLES IN 1911)

BOUNDARY OF
NAVY YARD
1915

CHAPMAN
HOUSE

STATE
ROAD

Quarters C

NORWICH AND
WORCESTER
BRANCH OF THE
N.Y. - NEW HAVEN
& HARTFORD RAIL-
ROAD 1898

1915 WATERFR

PRESENT WATERFRONT PIERS

HISTORICAL MAP OF 1915. This map shows the original waterfront in 1915, with the T-shaped wharf and the first few buildings. The State Road was altered by Mamacoke Hamlet due to the

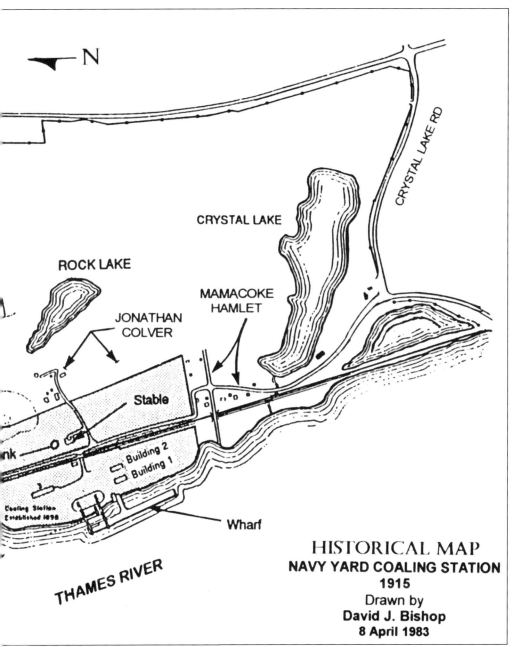

N

CRYSTAL LAKE RD

CRYSTAL LAKE

ROCK LAKE

MAMACOKE
HAMLET

JONATHAN
COLVER

Stable

nk

Building 2
Building 1

Cooling Station
Established 1898

Wharf

THAMES RIVER

HISTORICAL MAP
NAVY YARD COALING STATION
1915
Drawn by
David J. Bishop
8 April 1983

proximity of the railroad tracks. It is referred to as the upper road in chapter 2. The State Road was returned to its former placement by 1919 and ran parallel to the tracks.

VIEW FROM THE RIVER. The first few buildings can be seen along the waterfront in this early-1900s photograph. A water tower and stable, Building 6, can be seen behind Building 2. The coal pocket, built in 1900, is at the left. (Courtesy of SFL&M.)

Four

TRANSITION AND THE
FIRST SUBMARINES

Insufficient federal appropriations led to a gradual decline of the naval station, and at one point, it was recommended that the land be transferred back to the state of Connecticut. Although the majority of the men and supplies were transferred to other places, the station continued to provide limited service until 1898, when a coaling station was established.

In 1900, a modern coal-storage house, constructed of granite and steel, was completed. The coaling plant was extended in 1904, and on September 9, the plant was tested. The plant's coaling capacity was fixed at 393 tons per day. Many prominent ships refueled here, including the USS *Texas* in 1900. However, the expected flow of ships for refueling never materialized, and the New London station was listed for disposal in the naval appropriations bill submitted in 1912. Only the impassioned speech by Rep. Edwin Higgins of Norwich, Connecticut, could save the site.

It is believed that two submarines—the USS *Moccasin* (SS-5) and USS *Adder* (SS-3), both commissioned in 1903—put into New London in the early 1900s. This may have influenced the idea of establishing a submarine base here. (Note that the designation SS for submarines was not used until July 17, 1920, but is now used on those commissioned prior to that date for the sake of convenience.)

The monitor USS *Ozark*, acting as a tender, arrived at the station on October 18, 1915, with a division of submarines. Monitors were heavily armed cruisers with a very low freeboard and were particularly suitable as submarine tenders. The five submarines in this division were the G-1 (SS-19.5), G-2 (SS-27), D-1 (SS-17), D-2 (SS-18), and D-3 (SS-19). This odd-looking group of ships brought new activity to the waterfront. More submarines and their tenders followed. Among them was the USS *Fulton* (AS-1), which arrived on November 1, 1915. Her namesake, the USS *Fulton* (AS-11), was moored at State Pier in New London for many years.

NEW LONDON NAVY YARD IN BUSINESS. The battleship USS *Texas* takes on coal during the visit of the North Atlantic Squadron between July 24 and July 28, 1900. This squadron was composed of the battleships *New York*, *Indiana*, *Kearsarge*, *Kentucky*, and *Texas*. All received their coal from lighters (ships loaded with coal) in New London Harbor except the smaller *Texas*, which tied alongside the navy yard's T-shaped wharf. This photograph was taken for the Brown Hoist Company of Cleveland, Ohio, and was featured for several years in advertising by the manufacturer of the coal conveyers. (Courtesy of SFL&M.)

SHIPS TAKE ON COAL. Two ships wait to receive coal at the navy yard's T wharf in the early 1900s. (Courtesy of SFL&M.)

Rep. Edwin Higgins. When the navy yard was listed for disposal in 1912, Rep. Edwin Higgins made an impassioned speech, sparing the yard. (Courtesy of SFL&M.)

A Class Submarines. The USS *Moccasin* (SS-5), to the right, reportedly arrived at the navy yard in the early 1900s. In this photograph, the *Moccasin* and the *Shark* (to the left, along the pier) and three other A Class submarines are docked at the Electric Boat and Holland Torpedo Boat Company's basin in New Suffolk, New York. (Courtesy of SFL&M.)

USS SEAL (G-1). One of the first submarines to be stationed at the navy yard was the USS *Seal* (G-1) in 1915, shown here in the Thames River. The G-1 was the first submarine built under contract with Simon Lake, whose shipbuilding company was located in Bridgeport, Connecticut. Built in Newport News, Virginia, the G-1 was the first "even keel" submarine in the U.S. Navy. Prior to its development, submarines would submerge bow first, followed by the stern, "porpoise style." (Courtesy of SFL&M.)

CREW OF SUBMARINE G-1. Crew members appear on the deck of the USS *Seal* (G-1), docked at the navy yard in 1915. (Courtesy of SFL&M.)

USS OZARK AND SUBMARINES. The submarine tender USS *Ozark* arrived at the naval station in 1915 with submarines G-1, G-2, D-1, D-2, and D-3. (Courtesy of SFL&M.)

EARLY SUBMARINES. This view, taken from the second floor of Building 1, looks west across the T wharf. The four submarines docked are D and G Class boats and were among the first to be home ported at the site. From the foreground are the USS *Salmon* (D-3), USS *Narwhal* (D-1), USS *Turbot* (G-3), and USS *Thrasher* (G-4). Several small boats can be seen in the icy waters. (Courtesy of SFL&M.)

USS FULTON (AS-1). The first U.S. Navy ship to be built as a submarine tender was the USS *Fulton*, which arrived at the naval station in November 1915. (Courtesy of SFL&M.)

Five

THE SUBMARINE BASE

The submarine base assumed its permanent status on June 21, 1916. Cdr. Yates Stirling received orders from the acting secretary of the navy, Franklin D. Roosevelt, to assume command of the New London submarine flotilla, with additional duty in command of the submarine base and school.

On December 1, 1915, the station consisted of two old brick storehouses (Buildings 1 and 2), a brick barracks about 213 feet long and 40 feet wide (Building 3), a coal-storage shed, a few frame buildings, and a badly deteriorated T-shaped coal pier. Upon arrival of the boats at the yard, it became necessary to provide stowage ashore for the various supplies carried on board, and storehouses were built under the old coal pockets, which were a part of the coaling station plant. A severe fire on January 10, 1916, practically destroyed these buildings and the dock and necessitated additional construction at the same time as the establishment of the base ashore.

After the arrival of Commander Stirling, activity at the base steadily increased. On July 1, 1916, a school for the instruction of submarine officers began, using Building 3. The D Class boats were in active operation and were used as training boats. (Note that the first submarines, due to their small size, were referred to as boats and not ships. Submarines are still affectionately referred to as "boats," although the largest of them exceed 18,000 tons.)

In September 1916, a naval order established a tentative complement consisting of 76 men whose duties were to "assist submarines in routine repairs and to perform such jobs of construction and remodeling on the base proper as were within its scope."

FIRST COMMANDING OFFICER. Cdr. Yates Stirling took command of the New London flotilla, the submarine base, and the school on June 21, 1916. (Courtesy of SFL&M.)

OFFICERS GRADUATE. The first submarine school officers class graduation occurred in 1916. This photograph was taken in front of Building 3. (Courtesy of SFL&M.)

OFFICERS AND ENLISTED MEN. Students at the submarine school stand in formation at the south end of Building 3 in 1918. (Courtesy of SFL&M.)

ELEVATED RAILROAD TRACKS. Railroad cars loaded with coal climbed this elevated track past Building 1, en route to the coal pocket building. (Courtesy of SFL&M.)

T Wharf Buildings. The elevated railroad track in the previous photograph enters the south end of the coal pocket here. A storage building for submarine supplies and equipment lies beneath the coal-loading conveyor. (Courtesy of SFL&M.)

Submarine G-4 Crew Members. Standing on the deck of the G-4 are officers, chief petty officers, and crewmen. The executive officer was Lt. W. F. Calloway (fourth from left), and the commanding officer was Lt. P. F. Foster (fifth from left). (Courtesy of SFL&M.)

Six

WORLD WAR I

The country's entry into World War I caused the facilities at the base to be greatly expanded. Between October 1917 and October 1918, 81 buildings were completed or under construction, including the following: a new torpedo shop (Building 20); marine barracks (Building 22); mess hall (Building 25); hospital (Building 27); power house and machine shop, built on the foundation of the old coaling plant (Building 29); and battery shop (Building 31).

The waterfront was completely dredged to 22 feet (mean low water) and the old piers removed. Nine new finger piers and the quay wall were nearly complete by December 1918.

At this time, the submarine school occupied Building 3. Over 10,000 officers and enlisted men were trained for duty in the country's infant "silent service." During World War I, the submarine base serviced about 20 submarines, many of which had been stationed in the Azores and Ireland, providing anti-U-boat patrols.

RAILROAD DEPOT. The New York, New Haven, and Hartford Railroad built this depot to support military personnel arriving and departing the naval submarine base. This photograph was taken in 1918. (Courtesy of SFL&M.)

NEW FINGER PIERS. Once the old T-shaped wharf was removed, new piers were built to dock the growing fleet of submarines in August 1918. (Courtesy of SFL&M.)

SUBMARINE BASE FOUNDRY. Just inside the main gate is the base foundry, Building 37. The base hospital (left) and student officers' barracks (right) stand to the east of the railroad tracks passing over the main gate in this 1918 photograph. (Courtesy of SFL&M.)

LOWER BASE EXPANSION. Here, Building 1 is surrounded by new structures, a result of the 1918 expansion. The submarine R-21 is docked at one of the new piers. (Courtesy of SFL&M.)

ENLISTED MEN'S BARRACKS. In the left foreground is one of the new wooden enlisted men's barracks, Building 24. To the right is the laundry, Building 26, and to the far right is the hospital, Building 27. Closer to the river, the two wooden student officers' barracks, Building E (left) and Building F (right), appear in this April 14, 1918, photograph. (Courtesy of SFL&M.)

PASSING BY THE ENLISTED MEN'S BARRACKS. Groundwork begins in front of the enlisted men's barracks in this northward view. The water tower and bachelor officers' quarters are visible in the distance. (Courtesy of SFL&M.)

VIEW NORTH FROM LOWER BASE. The building to the right is Student Officers' Barracks E. Beyond it are the stable, water tower, and Bachelor Officers' Quarters D. (Courtesy of SFL&M.)

NEWSPAPER STAFF. The base newspaper, the *Journal*, had a staff of 14 in June 1918. Shown in no certain order are Arthur Wilkonson, Charles Riordan, George H. Densing, William C. Kastulja, Albert A. Baker, and Thomas F. McNevin. Not shown are Chief Petty Officer John Kennedy (editor and business manager), Ensign R. H. White (censor), J. C. Ford (advertising manager), J. L. Maydal (chief printer), and P. Wendell (cartoonist). (Courtesy of SFL&M.)

WATERFRONT AND POWER PLANT. In this 1919 northward view, various boats are docked at the new piers in front of the power plant. (Courtesy of SFL&M.)

LOWER BASE BUILDINGS. A number of new wooden fleet support buildings are shown in this 1919 photograph. (Courtesy of SFL&M.)

STUDENT OFFICERS' QUARTERS E. Above the student officers' quarters, some of the houses on the Colver property are visible. To the right is the hospital, Building 27. (Courtesy of SFL&M.)

VIEW OF THE WATERFRONT. This October 1918 panorama shows new buildings along the waterfront. In the background are, from left to right, the water tower, stable, student officers' and enlisted men's barracks, mess hall, and the houses of Mamacoke Hamlet. (Courtesy of SFL&M.)

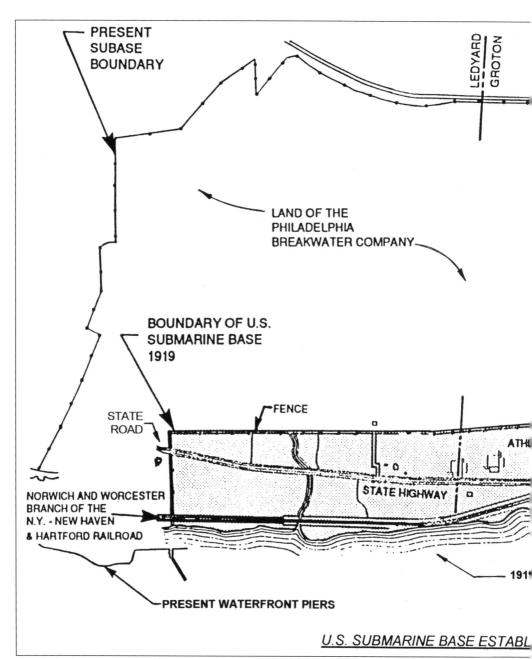

PRESENT
SUBASE
BOUNDARY

LEDYARD
GROTON

LAND OF THE
PHILADELPHIA
BREAKWATER COMPANY

BOUNDARY OF U.S.
SUBMARINE BASE
1919

FENCE

STATE
ROAD

ATH

STATE HIGHWAY

NORWICH AND WORCESTER
BRANCH OF THE
N.Y. - NEW HAVEN
& HARTFORD RAILROAD

191

PRESENT WATERFRONT PIERS

U.S. SUBMARINE BASE ESTABL

HISTORIC MAP OF 1919. The new construction that took place during World War I is evident in this map. As shown, the naval mine depot was placed a distance away from the populated

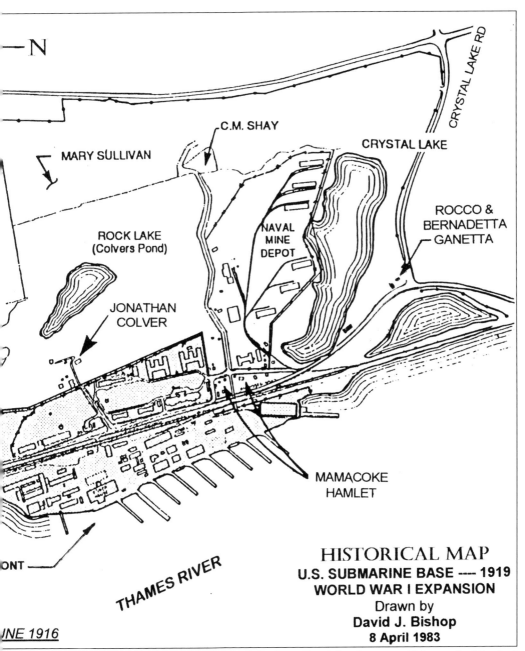

—N

MARY SULLIVAN

C.M. SHAY

CRYSTAL LAKE RD

CRYSTAL LAKE

ROCCO &
BERNADETTA
GANETTA

ROCK LAKE
(Colvers Pond)

NAVAL
MINE
DEPOT

JONATHAN
COLVER

MAMACOKE
HAMLET

THAMES RIVER

ONT

JNE 1916

HISTORICAL MAP
U.S. SUBMARINE BASE ---- 1919
WORLD WAR I EXPANSION
Drawn by
David J. Bishop
8 April 1983

areas and near Crystal Lake. The section of the State Road (in the area of Mamacoke Hamlet) that was removed in 1899 was replaced adjacent to the railroad tracks.

SUBMARINE BASE ADMINISTRATION. These two officers and six yeomanettes were employed at the administration office at the beginning of World War I. (Courtesy of SFL&M.)

SUBMARINE DOLPHINS. Submariners wear this insignia after they qualify in submarines. Enlisted men's insignias are silver, and officers' are gold. (Courtesy of the author.)

Seven

PEACE

After World War I, the base reverted to its prewar status. Construction of new submarines temporarily ended. Life and general activity continued at a much slower pace. It was time to apply the lessons learned from the war and explore solutions to the problems encountered.

The most notable achievement in the submarine service, in which this base took part, was the development of submarine safety, rescue, and salvage devices. On August 15, 1930, the navy's first submarine escape training tank was placed in operation. This tank contained a column of water more than 100 feet in height, with the necessary locks at different levels, and contained 250,000 gallons of water. It was a well-known structure and is still represented in the submarine base seal.

During the 1930s, in the period of the Great Depression, federal programs to aid the unemployed were incorporated at the submarine base. Several projects were completed by the WPA, and new structures were added as the base continued its expansion eastward, across the State Road. Buildings 83 and 84 were erected as the permanent site of the submarine school.

GUARDING THE MAIN GATE. These marines stand at their post while guarding the main gate to the submarine base. This gate led to the most secure area of the waterfront, the Lower Base, where submarines were docked. By the time this photograph was taken, on October 27, 1925, the submarine base was already expanding on the Upper Base, eastward of the State Road. (Courtesy of SFL&M.)

MAIN GATE DISTRIBUTION. The main concrete trench holding utilities distribution lines is being covered in this June 1920 photograph. Visible beneath the train trestle, marines guard the main gate to the Lower Base. In the distance is the majestic-looking stable, Building 6. (Courtesy of SFL&M.)

WATERFRONT DISTRIBUTION. A new high-pressure air system to the piers is constructed in 1919. Docked at the pier is a captured German submarine, UB-148. (Courtesy of SFL&M.)

GERMAN SUBMARINE UB-148. After World War I, this captured U-boat—along with U-117, UB-88, and UC-97 and accompanied by the submarine tender USS *Bushnell*—left England for New York. After a period of repairs, in June 1919 UB-148 arrived at the naval submarine base and was opened as a visitor site, in addition to being used for the ongoing bond drive. (Courtesy of SFL&M.)

SUBMARINES ALONG THE WATERFRONT. A number of S Class submarines are docked at the base in this 1925 photograph. (Courtesy of SFL&M.)

CREW INSPECTION. The crew of a submarine stands for inspection on a pier in the early 1920s. (Courtesy of SFL&M.)

NEW BUILDINGS. Under construction, these buildings are adjacent to the mine depot. Mines can be seen on the ground to the left. (Courtesy of SFL&M.)

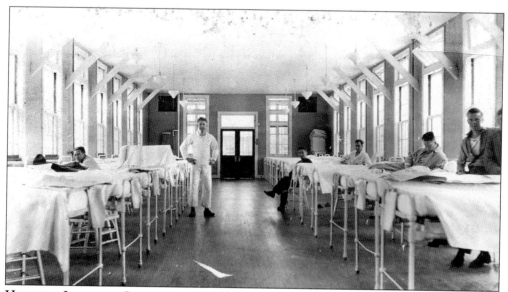

HOSPITAL INTERIOR. Some patients are shown in this view of the wooden hospital Building 27. (Courtesy of SFL&M.)

BUILDING 1 HEADQUARTERS. Originally a warehouse, Building 1 had become the submarine base headquarters, complete with window awnings and manicured lawns, by 1925. (Courtesy of SFL&M.)

CONTINGENT OF YEOMANETTES. "Yeomanettes," as they were popularly known, were female naval petty officers and primarily had secretarial and clerical duties. Some, however, served as translators, draftsmen, fingerprint experts, ship camouflage designers, and recruiting agents. Many honorably discharged yeomanettes were appointed to civil service positions in the same navy yards and stations where they had served in wartime. Entitled to veterans' preference for government employment, they provided a strong female presence in the navy's civilian staff through the decades after World War I. (Courtesy of SFL&M.)

PARKING LOT. Personnel working on the Lower Base took advantage of this large parking lot in the 1920s. This view looks north toward Buildings 1 and 2. (Courtesy of SFL&M.)

VIEW FROM LOWER BASE. This view of the main gate looks from the Lower Base to the State Road and the stable, Building 6, in 1925. To the right of the stable is the shed on the Colver property. (Courtesy of SFL&M.)

POWER PLANT AND MACHINE SHOP. This building was constructed on the granite foundation of the old coal pocket, visible at the structure's base. (Courtesy of SFL&M.)

PIERS FILLED WITH SUBMARINES. A number of S Class submarines are docked at the base in this 1925 photograph. (Courtesy of SFL&M.)

CORBITT TRUCK. The growing submarine base included a fleet of vehicles, including this truck, in September 1929. (Courtesy of SFL&M.)

SUBMARINE BASE AMBULANCE. This ambulance was among the base's government vehicles and was part of the medical department. (Courtesy of SFL&M.)

FIRST NAUTILUS TO APPROACH THE NORTH POLE. In 1954, Sir Hubert Wilkins and Donald Shepard look at a painting of Wilkins's submarine, the *Nautilus*, sailing near the Arctic ice pack in 1931. (Courtesy of SFL&M.)

O-12'S LAST VOYAGE. This submarine, built by the Lake Torpedo Boat Company of Bridgeport, Connecticut, undergoes conversion into Wilkins's *Nautilus* in 1930. (Courtesy of SFL&M.)

NAUTILUS AT THE PIER. Sir Hubert Wilkins's *Nautilus* takes on equipment and food at the submarine base during July and August 1931. (Courtesy of SFL&M.)

THE VOYAGE BEGINS. The *Nautilus* backs out from the pier as it begins its voyage to the North Pole in August 1931. The attempt to travel under the Arctic ice and reach the North Pole subsequently failed. The submarine was damaged during its trip across the Atlantic and suffered other breakdowns. After carrying out some experiments, Wilkins's team decided to end the trek, and the boat was sunk in a Norwegian fjord on November 20, 1931. (Courtesy of SFL&M.)

ESCAPE TRAINING TANK. Construction begins on a 100-foot training tank in 1930. Once completed and filled with water, it would be used to teach submariners how to escape a disabled boat. (Courtesy of SFL&M.)

ESCAPE TANK COMPLETED.
An elevator, seen on the left, brought submarine school students to the 25-foot and 50-foot levels from the top. Each level, as well as the bottom, contained locks (pressurized rooms) where students could enter the tank and rise to the surface, simulating an escape from a disabled submarine. A 12-foot-high, eight-sided room sat on top of the 100-foot tank. (Courtesy of SFL&M.)

FIRST CREW TO QUALIFY. These navy divers and submariners were the first to qualify in the escape tank. From left to right are the following: (first row) CTM Graham, GM1 Mavey, and BM2 Baker; (second row) MM1 Haynes, MM1 Hantsche, TM1 Robertson, and MM2 Drumm. (Courtesy of SFL&M.)

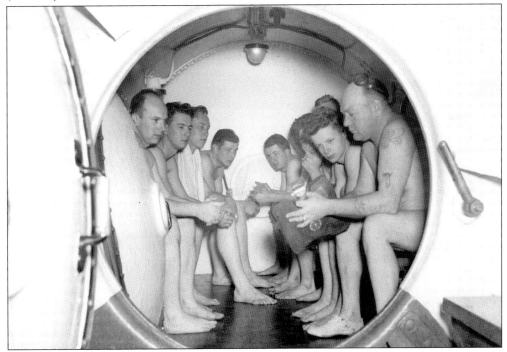

RECOMPRESSION CHAMBER. Submarine school enlisted students and instructors sit in a recompression chamber to experience being in a pressurized compartment. This procedure was necessary before entering the lock on the tank. (Courtesy of SFL&M.)

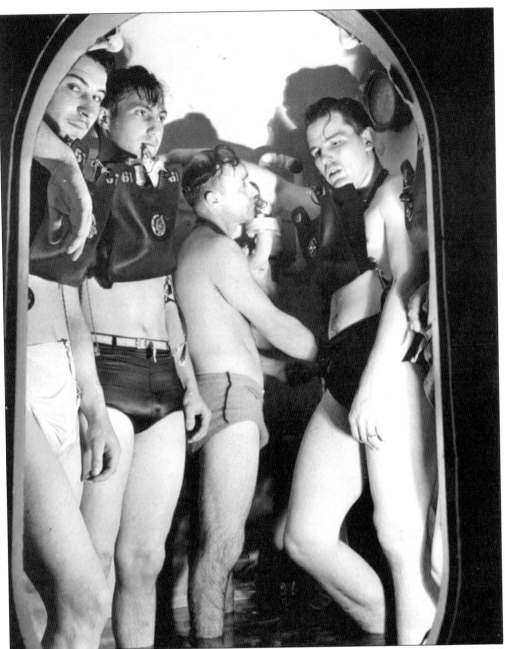

STUDENTS IN A PRESSURIZED LOCK. Most simulated escapes occurred from the 50-foot (depth) lock. Here, an instructor prepares to pressurize the lock in order to equal the tank's water pressure as students wait to exit. The students wear Momsen lungs, essentially re-breathers or second lungs. The devices relieved excess air pressure and acted as filters to remove exhaled carbon dioxide and return purified air to the wearers. Named after inventor Rear Adm. Charles B. Momsen, they were used in the tank until 1952. (Courtesy of SFL&M.)

EXITING THE LOCK. A student exits the pressurized lock, assisted by two instructors. Above the hatch is written "Ho-Ho-Ho." Students are trained to continuously say these words as they rise to avoid air embolism and other divers' hazards. (Courtesy of SFL&M.)

PREPARING TO ASCEND. This student readies to rise to the surface, accompanied by an instructor holding his belt. In 1961, the Steinke hood, named for inventor Lt. Harris E. Steinke, began usage in the submarine force. Made with a clear window, the hood was attached to a buoyant jacket and allowed the wearer to breath in a normal manner without incurring an air embolism. (Courtesy of SFL&M.)

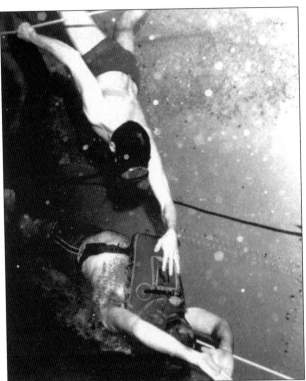

ASCENT BEGINS. Wearing a Steinke hood, a student begins his ascent, aided by an instructor. This view looks down from the surface. (Courtesy of SFL&M.)

STUDENTS ON THE SURFACE. These students, wearing Momsen lungs, have completed their ascent in the tank. (Courtesy of SFL&M.)

FORMER QUARRY. This aerial photograph, taken in 1937, shows the northern boundary of the submarine base (cleared area) and the quarry on the William Dampier property. (Courtesy of SFL&M.)

REFURBISHED MAIN GATE. New retaining walls with "U.S. Submarine Base" cast in their concrete added to the Lower Base's improved entrance. (Courtesy of SFL&M.)

VIEW LOOKING NORTH. The foundation of the old wooden enlisted men's barracks appears in the foreground of this 1937 photograph. To the right is the laundry, and to its right is the hospital—both soon to be razed and replaced with a new hospital, Building 86. (Courtesy of SFL&M.)

NEW EXPANSION BEGINS. This 1937 aerial photograph shows the razed wooden enlisted men's barracks. This is the site for the future submarine school, Buildings 83 and 84. The razed student officers' barracks (center left) is the future site of the Morton Drill Hall, Building 169. To the right is the student mess hall, soon to be demolished and replaced by the Dealey Recreation Center, Building 164. (Courtesy of SFL&M.)

NAVY DESTROYER AT PIER. Many surface ships visited the base. In this 1938 photograph, a destroyer is docked a short distance from Building 1, whose lawn is shown to the lower right. (Courtesy of SFL&M.)

VIEW LOOKING SOUTH. The top of the escape training tank affords a full view of the waterfront and Thames River, looking toward Fisher's Island Sound, in September 1935. (Courtesy of SFL&M.)

THE HURRICANE OF 1938. This 15,000-gallon oil tank tore loose from its foundation on the pier and threatened damage to the USS *Cachalot* when the waves kept driving it closer to the submarine. This photograph was taken on September 22, 1938, the day after the hurricane hit. (Courtesy of SFL&M.)

BUILDING 1 ROOF GONE. The fierce hurricane that hit southern New England on September 21, 1938, damaged many buildings at the submarine base. This image shows the complete loss of the Building 1 roof and the damage to the Building 2 connecting bridge. At the height of the storm, flying slate shingles would have killed anyone in the line of fire. (Courtesy of SFL&M.)

No Pier to Be Seen. At the height of the hurricane, two submarines are tied to a pier that is now underwater. (Courtesy of SFL&M.)

Hurricane Aftermath. A partially sunken barge rests against a damaged pier on the day after the hurricane. (Courtesy of SFL&M.)

NEW SUBMARINE SCHOOL BUILDINGS. In this May 1, 1939, southward view, the student enlisted men's barracks, Building 83, is under construction in the center, and the rear of the submarine school administration building, No. 84, can be seen on the right. (Courtesy of SFL&M.)

HOSPITAL BEING RAZED. The wooden hospital, Building 27, makes way for its replacement, Building 86, in 1939. (Courtesy of SFL&M.)

NEARING COMPLETION. The submarine school headquarters, Building 84 (left), and student enlisted men's barracks, Building 83 (right), near completion in July 1939. (Courtesy of SFL&M.)

NEW HOSPITAL. Opened in 1940, the new submarine base hospital, Building 86, stands just to the north of Submarine School Building 84. (Courtesy of SFL&M.)

MARINE RAILWAY. Construction is well along on the marine railway at the south end of the base in June 1941. This photograph shows the buoyed track structure being hauled out. The marine railway was used to move submarines for repair. (Courtesy of SFL&M.)

FIRST TEST. The 2,100-ton USS *Bonita* (SS-165) was the first submarine to use the marine railway, in November 1941. (Courtesy of SFL&M.)

Eight

WORLD WAR II

World War II presented the base with the awesome task of servicing a submarine fleet that was undergoing unprecedented growth. Expansion provided additional barracks, officers' quarters, school buildings, repair shops, piers, a mess hall (Building 151), and a new hospital (Building 86). A large indoor swimming pool, movie theater (Building 164), gymnasium and drill hall (Building 169), and chapel were also erected.

During the war, more than 33,000 officers and enlisted men were trained at the base, which was now known throughout the world as *the* training facility and proving ground of the U.S. submarine force. Accounting for less than two percent of our total naval strength, this force was credited with sinking 55 percent of enemy shipping, more than all other forces combined.

PREPARING TORPEDOES. Sailors ready two torpedoes for loading aboard a submarine. (Courtesy of SFL&M.)

READY TO GO. Torpedoes are moved out of the shop en route to a submarine docked at a nearby pier. In the background are the power plant and escape training tank. (Courtesy of SFL&M.)

PREPARING FOR PATROL. An inspection occurs aboard the USS *Mackerel* (SS-204), shown at center. The USS *Marlin* (SS-205) is at the pier to the right. (Courtesy of SFL&M.)

SAYING GOODBYE. Wives and children bid farewell to husbands and fathers as the USS *Ray* (SS-271) readies to leave on patrol during World War II. (Courtesy of SFL&M.)

HEADED FOR THE NORTH ATLANTIC. Family members wave goodbye to their loved ones as they leave the pier. (Courtesy of SFL&M.)

SAFE RETURN. Crew members of the USS *Finback* (SS-230) look for family members as they arrive at the pier after a patrol. (Courtesy of SFL&M.)

HOME AT LAST. Dock personnel assist crew members with the lines that hold the submarine snug to the pier. Flags and symbols painted on the side of the submarine indicate enemy ships destroyed. (Courtesy of SFL&M.)

SUBMARINE IN DRY DOCK. After returning from a patrol, some submarines required repairs and were "hauled out" on the marine railway. (Courtesy of SFL&M.)

NEW BARRACKS. Construction is under way on Building 159, one of many new enlisted men's barracks built during the war. (Courtesy of SFL&M.)

NEARING COMPLETION. This enlisted men's barracks, Building 158, is nearly finished in May 1944. (Courtesy of SFL&M.)

VIEW LOOKING WEST. To the right are new enlisted men's barracks, sprawling their way up the hill behind Building 83. (Courtesy of SFL&M.)

MOORING AND DOCKING TRAINER. Submarine officer students observe a model submarine maneuvering into a berth at this submarine school training facility.

BACHELOR OFFICERS' QUARTERS. Building D, shown here in 1944, was built adjacent to the old stable in 1918. (Courtesy of SFL&M.)

BACHELOR OFFICERS' QUARTERS EXPANSION. New Buildings L, M, and 379 rise around the original bachelor officers' quarters, Building D, shown at center. The building to the right of the water tower is the chief petty officers' club, Building 125. (Courtesy of SFL&M.)

VIEW LOOKING SOUTH. Automobiles are parked on the future site of the Dealey Recreation Center, Building 164, in April 1944. The marine railway appears in the center background. The Japanese submarine, seen at right, is similar to one sunk at Pearl Harbor on the day of the attack. It sits on the site of the future Morton Drill Hall, Building 169. (Courtesy of SFL&M.)

AERIAL VIEW. New barracks can be seen at upper left. At lower center, construction begins on the Dealey Recreation Center and the Chapel on the Thames, Building 168. (Courtesy of SFL&M.)

DEALEY CENTER THEATER. The south end of the Dealey Recreation Center contains a large theater, capable of holding stage productions. Construction progresses in this September 1944 photograph. (Courtesy of SFL&M.)

RECREATION CENTER COMPLETED. Housed in the new recreation center were a theater, cafeteria, bank, library, telephone exchange, bowling alley, barbershop, lounge, and post office. (Courtesy of SFL&M.)

MORTON DRILL HALL. Groundwork is started on the Morton Drill Hall and Gymnasium, Building 169, in September 1944. (Courtesy of SFL&M.)

DRILL HALL COMPLETED. Named after Cdr. Dudley W. Morton, the hall served a number of uses for large gatherings. (Courtesy of SFL&M.)

CHAPEL ON THE THAMES. Built on the site of the former gas station and trading post, the submarine base chapel takes shape in this August 1944 photograph. The Dealey Center building is under construction beyond. The old State Road, now renamed Shark Boulevard, runs to the left of the chapel. (Courtesy of SFL&M.)

NEARING COMPLETION. The chapel roof and steeple are in place in September 1944. (Courtesy of SFL&M.)

NEW WAVES BARRACKS. In June 1944, construction begins for a new Waves (navy enlisted women) barracks, Building 161. The chief petty officers' club stands behind, and the nurses' quarters are below in the former Colver house. The building to the right is the fire chief's house. (Courtesy of SFL&M.)

SECURITY MEASURES. The base hospital, as well as the submarine school headquarters and enlisted men's barracks, is secured with sandbags during World War II. (Courtesy of SFL&M.)

NEW MESS HALL. All enlisted personnel took their meals here, at Enlisted Men's Subsistence Building 151. (Courtesy of SFL&M.)

HOMOJA HUTS. Military housing for families was sparse in these Quonset-type huts during the early days of the war. (Courtesy of SFL&M.)

NEW ON-BASE HOUSING. Construction begins on brick apartment houses for married personnel in June 1944. The golf course is on the left, along with the north boundary of the base (cleared area). At the peninsula at upper left, granite was loaded on barges. The quarry on the Dampier property is at the upper right. (Courtesy of SFL&M.)

VIEW LOOKING SOUTH. This photograph of the northern end shows the golf course and the old State Road (now Shark Boulevard) running the length of the base. Granite was loaded on barges at the landing at lower left. Note that the Lower Base (waterfront) ends in the distance. The granite landing and Lower Base would soon be connected with new bulkheads and a road. (Courtesy of SFL&M.)

NEW MAIN GATE. The submarine base expansion during the war saw the southern boundary encompass the Ganetta property at the corner of Shark Boulevard and Crystal Lake Road. The two-story Ganetta house is shown at center. The white house was moved here from the Mamacoke Hamlet. (Courtesy of SFL&M.)

DIESEL ENGINE STUDENTS. The submarine school involved all facets of submarine training. These students, taking a diesel engine class, pose in January 1943. (Courtesy of SFL&M.)

TELEPHONE EXCHANGE. Multiple telephone booths and an operator's station opened in Dealey Center in 1945. (Courtesy of SFL&M.)

TRAINING AT SEA. Crew members engage in gunnery training off the coast of Connecticut during World War II. (Courtesy of SFL&M.)

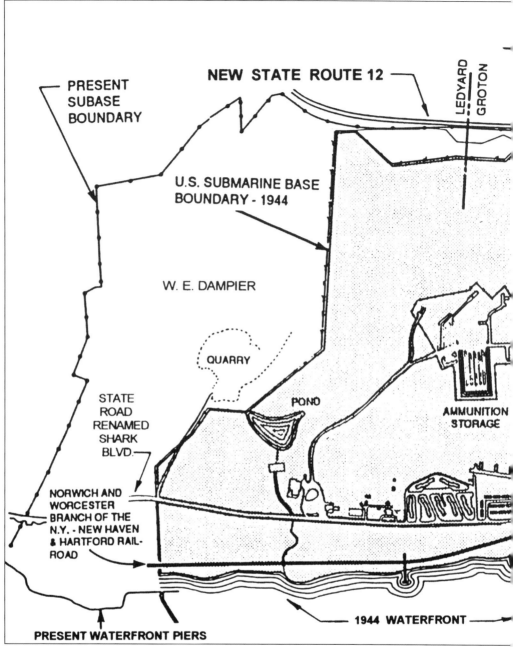

HISTORIC MAP OF 1944. The southern end of the base expanded to Crystal Lake Road, seen on the right, while the eastern boundary touched the new state Route 12, during the World War II period. The old State Road became military highway up to the northern boundary, and

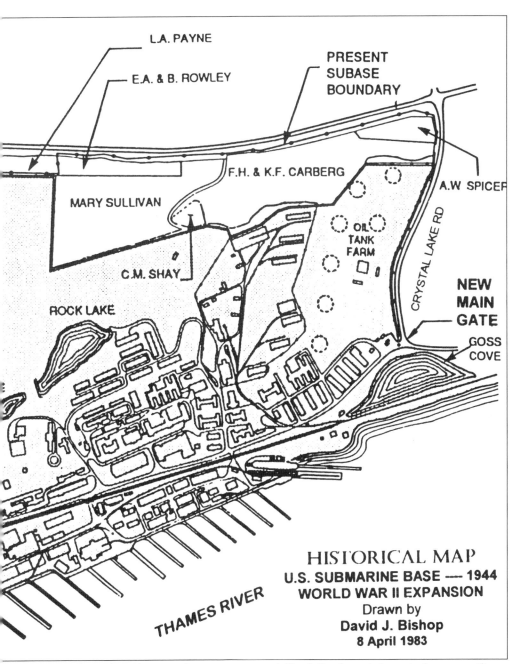

L.A. PAYNE

E.A. & B. ROWLEY

PRESENT
SUBASE
BOUNDARY

F.H. & K.F. CARBERG

A.W. SPICER

MARY SULLIVAN

OIL
TANK
FARM

CRYSTAL LAKE RD

NEW
MAIN
GATE

C.M. SHAY

ROCK LAKE

GOSS
COVE

THAMES RIVER

HISTORICAL MAP
U.S. SUBMARINE BASE —— 1944
WORLD WAR II EXPANSION
Drawn by
David J. Bishop
8 April 1983

the length along the submarine base was renamed Shark Boulevard. It again became military highway as it left the new main gate and proceeded south along the Thames River.

SUBMARINE BASE NEW LONDON SEAL. Incorporating the escape training tank and the USS *Nautilus* (SSN-571), the seal was designed in the late 1950s. Author David J. Bishop created this new artwork for public relations purposes in 1985.

Nine

PEACE AGAIN

Immediately after the close of World War II, it was evident that reduced appropriations would not permit keeping large numbers of submarines in service. Rather than scrap these boats, officials decided to preserve them in an inactive status. A reserve berthing area was provided west of the present golf course, where four submarine tenders and about 50 submarines were docked. The mothball fleet remained here until the 1950s.

HEADING OUT TO SEA. Submarine activity began to slow down after the war ended. Crews were reassigned to shore duty, and the navy found itself with excess submarines and other ships. (Courtesy of SFL&M.)

AERIAL VIEW LOOKING SOUTH. The railroad tracks, built during 1899, run along the original waterfront in this 1946 photograph. These tracks created the "Upper Base" to the left and the "Lower Base" to the right, terms that are still used today. Goss Cove is shown at the upper right, while Crystal Lake Road proceeds to the east to join the new state Route 12, located on the left. This area would soon have a new road and buildings erected on land fill behind new bulkheads. (Courtesy of SFL&M.)

AERIAL VIEW LOOKING NORTH. The war expansion is evident here. The waterfront would soon push northward to accommodate a fleet of excess submarines. (Courtesy of SFL&M.)

THE 16TH RESERVE FLEET. Two submarine tenders and about two dozen submarines are temporarily docked at the submarine base in 1946, awaiting construction of new piers. (Courtesy of SFL&M.)

FILL BEHIND BULKHEADS. A barge and crane begin work in preparation for construction of new bulkheads along the shoreline. Gravel and even old cars are used for fill in this March 1946 southward view. (Courtesy of SFL&M.)

NEW FINGER PIERS. Piers along the new bulkheads are completed in October 1946 and await the reserve fleet submarines. (Courtesy of SFL&M.)

NEW CONCRETE PIER. Once the reserve fleet submarines are docked at the finger piers, a new concrete pier, seen in the center, is completed to hold two new floating dry docks: ARD 5 and ARD 7. (Courtesy of SFL&M.)

MOTHBALLING BEGINS. In order to help preserve equipment on the reserve submarines, sailors encase guns and other deck items in plastic sheeting. (Courtesy of SFL&M.).

SUBMARINE BASE AERIAL VIEW. This July 1947 photograph shows the four boundaries of the base. Once the Dampier property was purchased, the northern boundary moved past the golf course to the present north gate. The new state Route 12 (top) secured the eastern boundary, and Crystal Lake Road (right) was the southern boundary. In this image, the reserve submarine fleet numbers 46 boats. (Courtesy of SFL&M.)

RESERVE SUBMARINES. Reserve fleet submarines are tied side by side at a finger pier. Deck equipment can be seen wrapped in plastic. (Courtesy of SFL&M.)

ARD 5 AND 7 DOCKED. Auxiliary repair dry docks are at their new concrete pier in 1947. These vessels have double walls that let in seawater so they can partially submerge. Submarines are led in the open stern, where they sit on previously prepared wooden blocks (cradles). The water is then pumped out of the double walls, and the ARD rises, exposing the entire submarine in a dry dock. (Courtesy of SFL&M.)

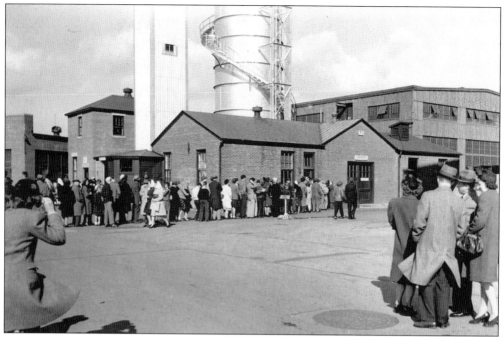

NAVY DAY VISITORS. Families and area citizens attend a Navy Day open house in 1946. One group prepares to enter Building 70, the structure at the base of the escape training tank. (Courtesy of SFL&M.)

A BOAT RIDE ALONG THE WATERFRONT. Visitors are treated to a ride along the base shoreline during this Navy Day open house. (Courtesy of SFL&M.)

WAITING TO BE RAZED. Stately Building 5 served as the security office (guardhouse) and stood adjacent to the original Lower Base main gate. Here, it is being readied for demolition in 1947. The foundry, Building 37, is shown behind. (Courtesy of SFL&M.)

BOXING MATCHES. One of the "in-season" sports was boxing, with matches held in the Morton Hall Gymnasium, Building 169. (Courtesy of SFL&M.)

FAMILY HEALTH. A doctor at the base hospital, Building 86, talks with a patient in 1946. (Courtesy of SFL&M.)

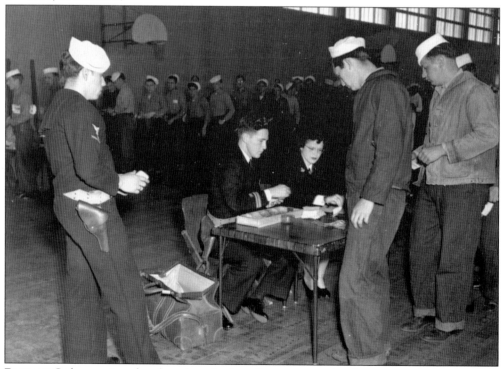

PAYDAY. Sailors stationed at the submarine base line up to receive their pay in the Morton Hall Gymnasium in 1946. (Courtesy of SFL&M.)

Ten

THE NUCLEAR AGE OF THE 1950S AND BEYOND

When the development of an atomic-powered submarine picked up speed in the late 1940s, the submarine base entered a new phase. Anticipating the effects brought on by advances in technology, construction was started and manpower requirements were increased. New construction in the 1950s and 1960s included a complex of new brick barracks, off-crew training facilities, a large enlisted men's club, and major addition to the officers' quarters and new piers. In the 1980s, construction included a marine barracks, submarine school buildings, a home for the historic ship USS *Nautilus* (SSN-571), and the Submarine Force Library and Museum, located at Goss Cove.

The administrative organization also changed, and in June 1964, the medical research laboratory and base hospital were removed to form the Submarine Medical Center. In June 1968, the Naval Submarine School changed from an activity to a command, becoming the longest single tenant on the base. In February 1974, the Naval Submarine Support Facility was established as a separate command. These and other former activities now have their own responsibility and commanding officer or officer-in-charge.

The submarine base command is responsible for maintaining facilities to support these tenant commands and the submarines assigned here. The area of the base now encompasses 687 acres. Manpower consists of approximately 7,500 military members, 1,000 contractors, and over 1,400 civilian employees.

Could the citizens of Connecticut and New London expect such results and rewards from their gift of 112 acres of land to the navy back in 1868?

MAIN GATE. A sign on the guard booth states, "No Visitors Allowed" in this photograph during the winter of 1950. The white building to the right was moved from Mamacoke Hamlet and houses the security officer. The Ganetta house at far right is in use as the security office. (Courtesy of SFL&M.)

USS LOOKOUT II. This small boat, adjacent to Rock Lake (formally Colver's Pond), was used for periscope training in a nearby submarine school building. (Courtesy of SFL&M.)

PRES. HARRY S. TRUMAN. The president inspects the troops at the main gate before proceeding to the Electric Boat Company on June 14, 1952. The occasion was the keel laying of the first nuclear-powered ship, the submarine USS *Nautilus* (SSN-571). The president welded his initials on the keel at the ceremony. (Courtesy of SFL&M.)

AERIAL VIEW LOOKING NORTH. The main gate (bottom) has acquired new buildings in this October 1963 photograph. The white house has moved to a grassy area and would later move again near the officers' club, where it remains. The Ganetta house is still in use as the security office. (Courtesy of SFL&M.)

COMMISSIONED AND WARRANT OFFICERS' MESS. Perched high on a rocky outcropping, the officers' club boasts a commanding view of the river and golf course. (Courtesy of SFL&M.)

SUBMARINES' NEW SHAPE. These World War II–era submarines have taken new streamlined shapes in this 1960s view. The reserve submarine fleet piers (top) are being dismantled. (Courtesy of SFL&M.)

VIEW LOOKING WEST. New enlisted men's barracks, located at the east boundary along state Route 12, are shown completed in 1961. Crystal Lake Road is to the left. (Courtesy of SFL&M.)

CHANGE OF COMMAND. The Naval Submarine Base Band plays for a change-of-command ceremony aboard the submarine USS *Angler* (SS-240), right, in 1965. The submarine in the center is the USS *Sea Owl* (SS-405). (Courtesy of SFL&M.)

NEW DRY DOCK. Repair dry dock medium (RDM4) arrived in the early 1980s and is shown with a fast-attack submarine undergoing repairs. (Courtesy of SFL&M.)

UPHILL EXPANSION. Seen in the upper right of this 1989 photograph are, from left to right, a new hospital (Building 449), water tower, and enlisted men's barracks. A marina and sailing club are located at the pier at the upper left. (Courtesy of SFL&M.)

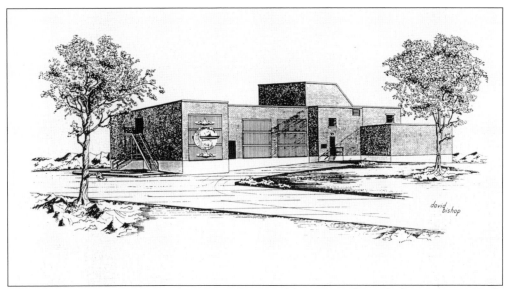

PENNINGTON HALL. Naval Submarine School Building 152, also called Pennington Hall, houses a number of ship control trainers mounted on gimbals, simulating diving and surfacing a submarine. This artwork was created by the author.

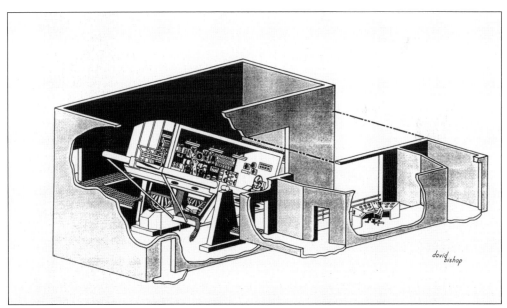

TRIGGER CONTROL TRAINER. Once housed in Pennington Hall, this diesel boat trainer, comparable to the submarine USS *Trigger* (SS-564), was reassembled as a static display at the Submarine Museum. This artwork was created by the author.

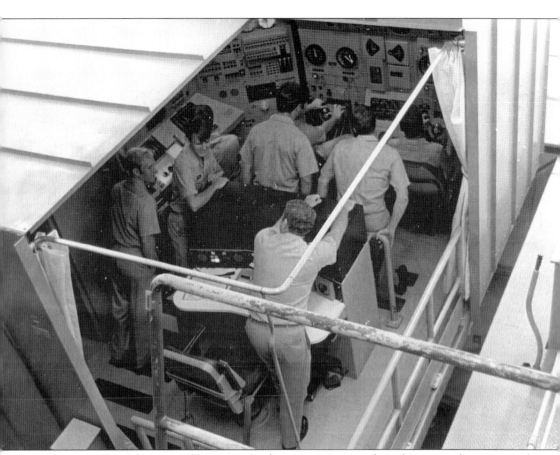

NUCLEAR SHIP CONTROL TRAINER. Students operate a nuclear ship control trainer at the Naval Submarine School. These devices replaced training that students performed on diesel submarines while at sea. (Courtesy of the author.)

DAMAGE CONTROL TRAINER. Building 485 contains a simulated submarine interior. Water is released through controlled leaks, and students use their learned skills to stop the leaks. (Courtesy of the author.)

IMPORTANT TASK. This student applies a patch to a leak on a high-pressure water pipe. Water in a submarine affects buoyancy, and stopping leaks can prevent a submarine from sinking. (Courtesy of the author.)

SUBMARINE FORCE LIBRARY AND MUSEUM. Originally established as the Submarine Library at the Electric Boat Company in 1955, the entire collection was donated to the navy in April 1964 and relocated to Building 83. The name was officially adopted in 1969. (Courtesy of the author.)

GOSS COVE MUSEUM SITE. This February 1984 view, looking south, shows the area at Goss Cove that would become the new home of the museum and the permanent berth of the USS Nautilus Memorial. (Courtesy of the author.)

NAUTILUS AND MUSEUM COMPLEX. When the USS *Nautilus* (SSN-571) was decommissioned in 1980, plans were formulated to preserve the first nuclear-powered submarine as a memorial and tourist attraction. Groton, the birthplace of the *Nautilus*, was chosen, and funds were raised to construct a berth and museum building at Goss Cove. Construction is under way in this October 1984 photograph. (Courtesy of the author.)

MUSEUM NEARS COMPLETION. The museum building and pier take shape alongside Goss Cove and the Thames River in June 1985. (Courtesy of the author.)

FLEET BOAT MODEL. Assembly begins on the 52-foot model of a USS *Gato* (SS-212) Class submarine. The highly detailed model is hung at eye level with the second-floor mezzanine and has cutaway sections so visitors can look inside. Battle flags, made by crew members of submarines during World War II, are lined up prior to being hung from the ceiling. (Courtesy of the author.)

WORK PROGRESSES. The second-floor mezzanine is bordered on the left by a backlit photograph wall of submarine activities. The USS *Nautilus* room is at the far end, overlooking the submarine at its berth. (Courtesy of the author.)

TURTLE RE-CREATION. A full-size model of the country's first submarine, built in 1775 in Saybrook, is moved into the museum. This working submarine, on loan by the Connecticut River Museum in Essex, was designed by Joe Leary and built by Fred Frese. In 1976, it was used in the Connecticut River to re-create the 1776 attack on Adm. Richard Howe's flagship, the HMS *Eagle*, in New York Harbor. (Courtesy of the author.)

FLEET BALLISTIC MISSILE SUBMARINE HATCH. This hatch was part of the deck structure of a fleet ballistic missile submarine. Once opened, it allowed a missile to be ejected. (Courtesy of the author.)

JULES VERNE'S *20,000 LEAGUES BENEATH THE SEA*. Author David J. Bishop paints a 12- by 12-foot mural of a page taken from the novel *20,000 Leagues beneath the Sea* in March 1986. The mural is located above the interior entrance to the museum. (Courtesy of the author.)

FICTITIOUS *NAUTILUS*. This model of the submarine *Nautilus*, depicted in Walt Disney's 1954 movie *20,000 Leagues beneath the Sea*, was built by author David J. Bishop in 1985–1986 and donated to the museum. The 11-foot-long model hangs in the foyer, just below the mural of an engraving from Verne's book. (Courtesy of the author.)

NAUTILUS ARRIVES. The *Nautilus* was decommissioned in California on March 3, 1980. The following years saw it reconfigured to accept visitors. It was designated a national landmark on May 20, 1982. In this photograph, a tugboat ties up to the *Nautilus* in the Atlantic Ocean before its last voyage to the submarine base on July 6, 1985. (Courtesy of the author.)

JOURNEY UPRIVER. Tied to two tugboats, the *Nautilus* approaches the railroad and Gold Star bridges on its trip up the Thames River. (Courtesy of the author.)

Nautilus Passes Its Future Home. Accompanied by a flotilla of pleasure and navy vessels, the *Nautilus* passes the pier and museum building, still under construction. (Courtesy of the author.)

Finally Home. The *Nautilus* was moved from a pier on the submarine base to its permanent berth in October 1985. Long struts are attached to the submarine to keep it a controlled distance from the pier and allow up-and-down movement with the tide. (Courtesy of the author.)

NAUTILUS AND MUSEUM COMPLEX. This ink drawing, created by author David J. Bishop, shows the complex from the river. The artwork was used in the April 20, 1986, grand opening brochure. A glass-enclosed deckhouse was installed at the bow, instead of the small covering shown, to provide visitors protection from the elements. (Artwork by the author.)

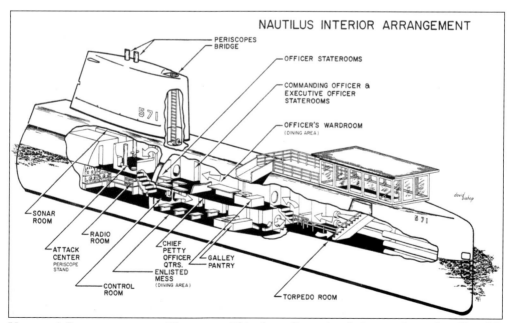

VISITORS' ROUTE THROUGH NAUTILUS. This three-dimensional drawing by author David J. Bishop shows the route taken by visitors. A special double stairway was installed at the bow, inside the glass-enclosed deckhouse, to allow easier maneuvering below. (Artwork by the author.)

SUBMARINE BASE AND ENVIRONS. This 1989 view, looking west, reveals the new off-base housing, Trident Park, at lower left. The Nautilus Memorial, now called the Historic Ship Nautilus, and the museum are shown at left center. Across the Thames River at upper left are the buildings of Connecticut College and the U.S. Coast Guard Academy in New London. (Courtesy of SFL&M.)

SILENT SERVICE. This illustration by author David J. Bishop includes many components of the U.S. Submarine Force and U.S. Naval Submarine Base New London.

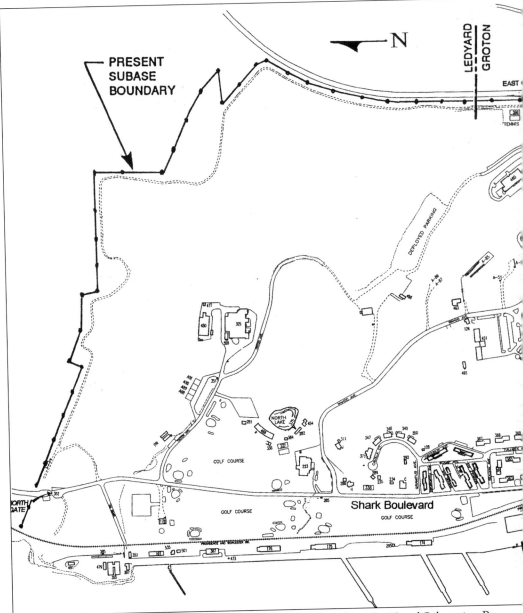

HISTORIC MAP OF 1988. This map shows the tremendous growth at the Naval Submarine Base New London over the 120 years since the 1868 purchase of land for a navy yard. This expansion

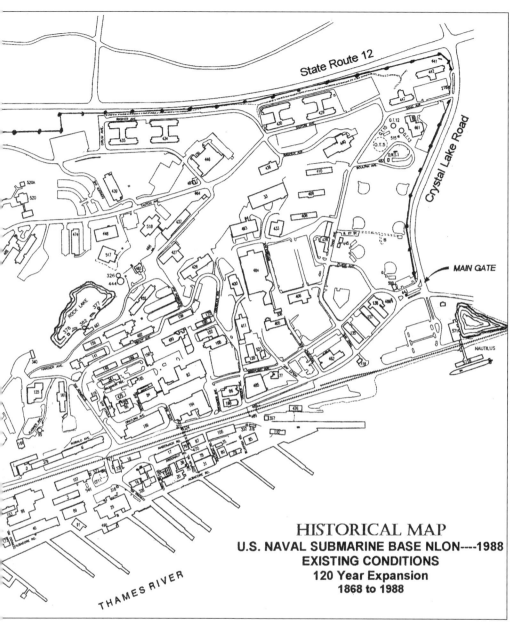

HISTORICAL MAP
U.S. NAVAL SUBMARINE BASE NLON----1988
EXISTING CONDITIONS
120 Year Expansion
1868 to 1988

continues to the present day, with new barracks, submarine school training buildings, and other infrastructure not seen here.

SUBMARINE CAPITAL OF THE WORLD. This sign, in the shape of the USS *Groton* (SSN-694), proclaims Groton, Connecticut, as the "Submarine Capital of the World." It stood for many years along Interstate 95 in Groton. (Courtesy of the author.)

NEW SIGN. In September 2004, on the 50th anniversary of the commissioning of the USS *Nautilus* (SSN-571), a sign in the shape of *Nautilus* was erected in place of the previous one. (Courtesy of the author.)